WHERE IS MY TOWN?

by Robin Nelson

first step nonfiction

Lerner Publications Company · Minneapolis

I live in a **town.**

A town is a group of
neighborhoods.

I live in my town with my family.

I go to school in my town.

I shop in my town.

I play in my town.

My town is in my state.

There are towns all
over the world.

Some towns have a lot of people but very little land.

These towns are called
cities.

Some towns have more land
and fewer people.

These towns are called
suburbs.

Some towns have a lot of
land and not a lot of people.

These towns are in the **country.**

Where is my town?

My town is in my state,
where I live with my family.

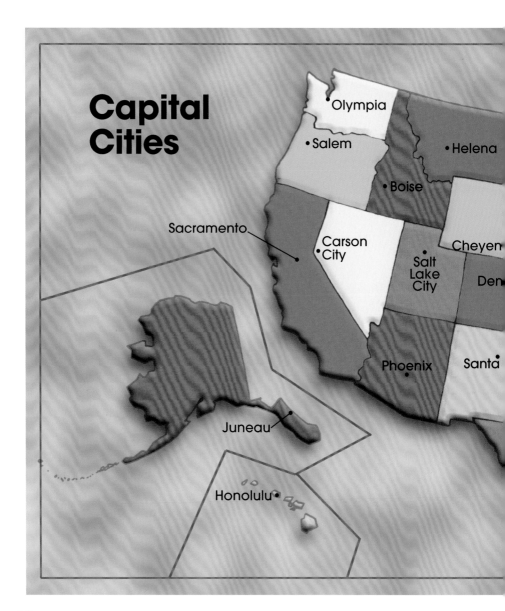

Capital Cities

Olympia

Salem

Helena

Boise

Sacramento

Carson City

Cheyen

Salt Lake City

Den

Phoenix

Santa

Juneau

Honolulu

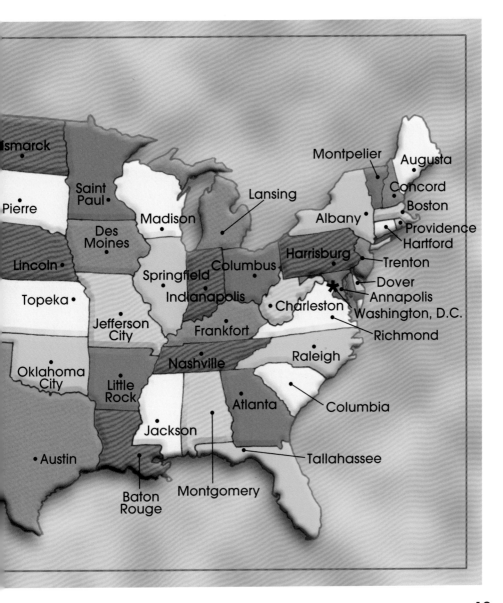

Town Facts

⭐ Saint Augustine, Florida, is the oldest city in the United States. Spaniards founded it in 1565.

⭐ Jamestown, Virginia, was the first permanent British settlement in North America. About 100 colonists established it in 1607.

⭐ The city with the largest population in the world is Tokyo, Japan.

⭐ The U.S. city with the most people is New York City.

The most common town names in the United States are:
1. Fairview
2. Midway
3. Oak Grove
4. Franklin
5. Riverside
6. Centerville
7. Mount Pleasant
8. Georgetown
9. Salem
10. Greenwood

Glossary

 cities – places where many people live and work. A city is a large town.

 country – an area away from a city where few people live

 neighborhoods – homes and people who live around you

 suburbs – areas on or close to the outer edge of a city

 town – a place where people live and work. A town is smaller than a city.

Index

The photographs in this book are reproduced through the courtesy of: © Corbis Royalty Free, front cover, p. 16; © D. Yeske/Visuals Unlimited, pp. 2, 22 (bottom); © Patrick Cone, pp. 3, 12, 22 (middle); © Trip/H. Rogers, p. 4; © Tom Edwards/Visuals Unlimited, p. 5; © David Young-Wolff/Stone, p. 6; © Mark Gibson/Visuals Unlimited, p. 7; © Joseph Sohm/Corbis, p. 8; © Wolfgang Kaehler, pp. 9, 11, 13, 14, 22 (top, second from top, second from bottom); © M. Bryan Ginsberg, p. 10; © John Green/Visuals Unlimited, p. 15; © Gerard Fritz/Photo Agora, p. 17.

Lerner Publications Company
A division of Lerner Publishing Group, Inc.
241 First Avenue North
Minneapolis, MN 55401 U.S.A.

Website address: www.lernerbooks.com

Library of Congress Cataloging-in-Publication Data

Nelson, Robin, 1971–
    Where is my town? / by Robin Nelson.
       p.   cm. — (First step nonfiction)
    Includes index.
    ISBN-13: 978–0–8225–0190–9 (lib. bdg. : alk. paper)
    ISBN-10: 0–8225–0190–2 (lib. bdg. : alk. paper)
    1. Cities and towns—Juvenile literature. 2. City and town life—Juvenile literature.
3. Family life—Juvenile literature. [1. Cities and towns.]
I. Title. II. Series.
HT119.N45 2002
307.76—dc21
                                               2001000965

Manufactured in the United States of America
11 – PC – 9/1/13